The Green
Scene

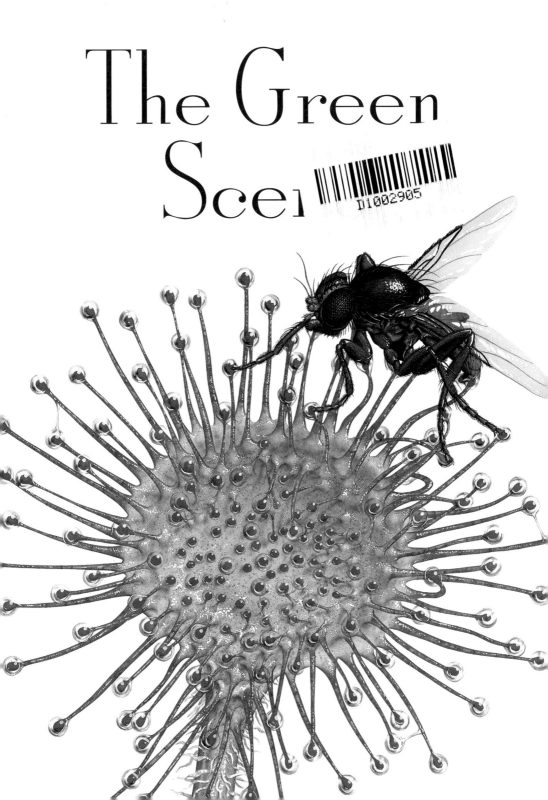

Contents

Features

Recognizing parts of our words that come from Greek or Roman words can help you understand science text. Find out more on page 5.

Catch a bug or worm! Turn to **Make a Berlese Funnel** on page 19 and observe the tiny living things that keep our planet working.

Giant pandas are a very endangered species, so the birth of a panda cub is a special event. Read all about it in **Panda Baby** on page 25.

Believe it or not, there are ecosystems everywhere, even in cities. You might be surprised at what you can see in **City Living** on page 28.

How is a tapeworm like a mosquito?

Visit www.rigbyinfoquest.com
for more about ECOLOGY.

What Is Ecology?

Ecology is the study of the way living things, or **organisms**, interact with their environments. When ecologists study an animal, they study the food it eats, the environment it lives in, the climate around it, the air it breathes, the water it drinks, and the predators that stalk it. Ecologists study everything that affects an animal.

Humans share Earth with many types of plants and animals. Sometimes, however, human activities destroy or pollute the habitats that plants and animals live in. This can affect plants or animals in unpredictable ways. Ecologists try to understand the connections between organisms, including humans, and their environment.

Researchers sometimes take blood samples so they can find out more about an animal.

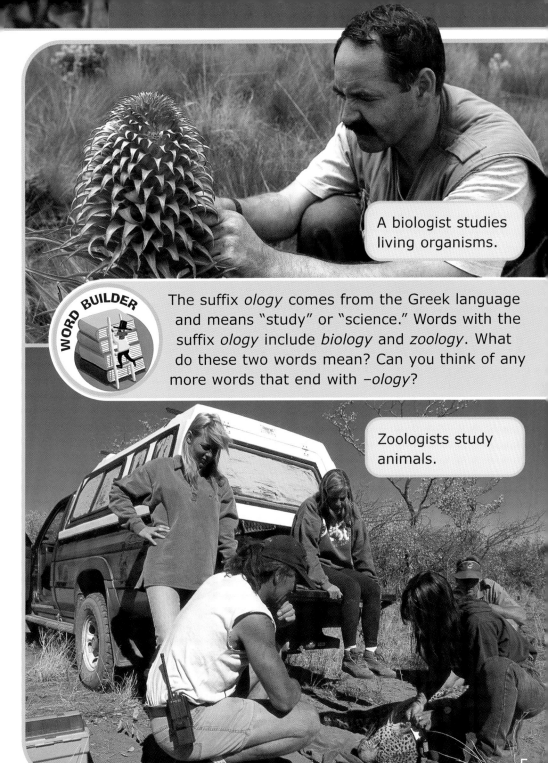

A biologist studies living organisms.

WORD BUILDER

The suffix *ology* comes from the Greek language and means "study" or "science." Words with the suffix *ology* include *biology* and *zoology*. What do these two words mean? Can you think of any more words that end with *–ology*?

Zoologists study animals.

The Living World

A biosphere is a whole world of living things. Scientists call Earth Biosphere 1. Our biosphere is divided into biomes.

Biomes

Biomes are large areas that have particular kinds of plants and animals and a particular climate of light, water, temperature, and winds. Our world's biomes can be classified into five major groups—aquatic, deserts, forests, grasslands, and tundra. Each of these major biome groups have several kinds of biomes within them.

Tropical rain forest

Grasslands

Desert

For example, the forests biome group includes two kinds of tropical forest biomes and temperate forest biomes. The aquatic biome group includes marine and freshwater biomes. Oceans, the marine biome, are the world's largest biome—they cover 71% of Earth's surface.

Temperate deciduous forest

Tundra

Temperate coniferous forest

Aquatic (marine)

Populations and Ecosystems

A group of animals or plants of the same species living in the same area is called a population. A pack of hyenas living on a savanna in Africa, for example, is a population. Populations of animals change over time.

A community is a group of two or more populations that interact. The hyenas interact with the lions, zebras, vultures, and wildebeests that also live on the savanna. This is a community of animals.

Factors That Increase Populations	Factors That Decrease Populations
Birth	Death from natural causes
Good weather, lots of food	Bad weather, natural disasters
Few or no predators	Large number of predators
Less competition for food	More competition for food

An ecosystem (short for *ecological system*) includes all the populations living in a particular area plus the nonliving environment. The ecosystem of the African savanna includes all living things from the tiniest insect to the largest elephant, all the plants, the waterholes, the soil, and the amount of wind, rain, and sunshine.

Controlled Environments

Scientists sometimes do experiments on ecosystems to see what happens if they change one **variable.** For example, they might remove one population and see what happens to the other populations. Scientists like to be able to control the environment so they can change one variable at a time.

One famous controlled environment is called Biosphere 2. Biosphere 2 is a huge glass laboratory just north of Tucson, Arizona. Biosphere 2 is a totally self-contained ecosystem. It contains six biomes— a rain forest, a desert, a savanna, a wetland, an ocean, and an agro-forestry biome, where mature trees are grown in special conditions.

Biosphere 2

Wetland

Ocean

Tropical rain forest

Savanna

IN FOCUS

Mainland Islands

New Zealand's Karori Wildlife Sanctuary is an example of a "mainland island." This area of forest exists in the middle of a city, but it's isolated like an island by a specially designed 5-mile fence. Pests and predators are unable to climb over, burrow under, or wriggle through the fence. Karori Wildlife Sanctuary is giving the rare and endangered plants and animals inside the "island" a chance to flourish.

Desert

Agro-forestry

Laboratories and offices

Food Chains

All living things must interact to survive. One of the most important ways they interact is by eating and being eaten. Scientists show how food energy passes from one living thing to another by using a diagram called a food chain. All living things have a place in a food chain.

A Food Chain

Bears ← Big fish ← Small fish ← Water insects ← Water plants

It takes many insects to feed one small fish, many small fish to feed one big fish, and many big fish to feed one bear.

In a food chain, energy moves from one living thing, as it is eaten, to another living thing. In the example on these pages, the bear is at the top of the food chain because nothing eats the bear—until it dies. Going up a food chain toward the top, the animal populations get smaller as the animals get bigger in size.

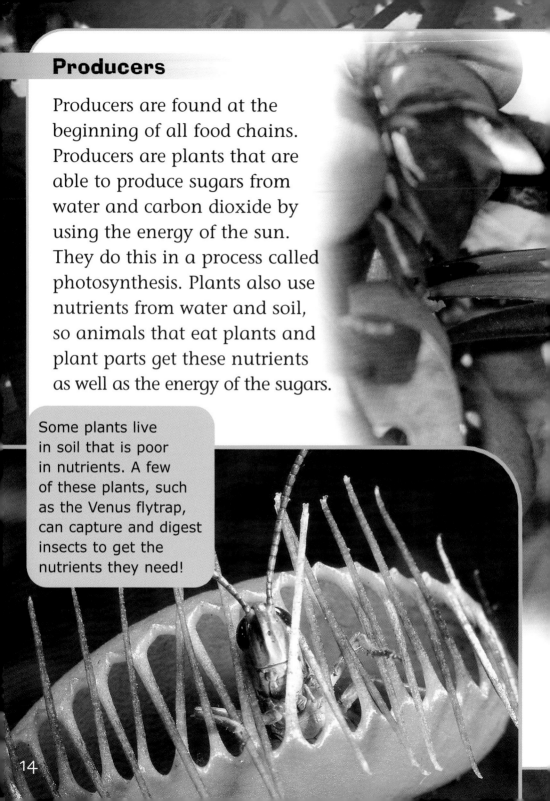

Producers

Producers are found at the beginning of all food chains. Producers are plants that are able to produce sugars from water and carbon dioxide by using the energy of the sun. They do this in a process called photosynthesis. Plants also use nutrients from water and soil, so animals that eat plants and plant parts get these nutrients as well as the energy of the sugars.

Some plants live in soil that is poor in nutrients. A few of these plants, such as the Venus flytrap, can capture and digest insects to get the nutrients they need!

Some plants produce tasty fruit so that birds and animals will eat it, helping to spread the plants' seeds.

In every food chain, energy moves from the sun to plants and then from plants to animals. Plants turn the sun's energy into chemical energy—food—that animals can use.

Consumers

Consumers are animals that use the food energy of producers or other consumers. They must consume plants or other animals to survive. Primary consumers, also known as herbivores, eat plants. Secondary consumers are carnivores, or meat-eaters, that eat other animals. Secondary consumers might be predators, which catch and kill their prey, or scavengers, which eat dead or dying animals. There are many animals that eat both plants and other animals. They are called omnivores.

IN FOCUS

Mosquito

Lappetfaced vultures are scavengers that feast on leftovers.

What's Eating You?

Many animals use humans for food energy. Millions of mites and bacteria live on every person, eating dead skin cells. Many insects, such as fleas and mosquitoes, like to chow down on human blood. All these animals are called parasites.

Lions are excellent hunters that are able to catch zebras and other large prey. They are carnivores.

The kinkajou is a fruit-eating herbivore in South America.

How is a tapeworm like a mosquito?

Visit **www.rigbyinfoquest.com**
for more about **ECOLOGY.**

SITESEEING

• PLANTS & ANIMALS •

Decomposers

Decomposers eat dead animals, dead plants, plant parts such as fallen leaves, and even animal droppings. Decomposers are the living things that break down other living and nonliving things into nutrients and energy to be reused by plants. Decomposers make a complete cycle possible. Fungi, bacteria, earthworms, and many insects such as scarab beetles are all decomposers.

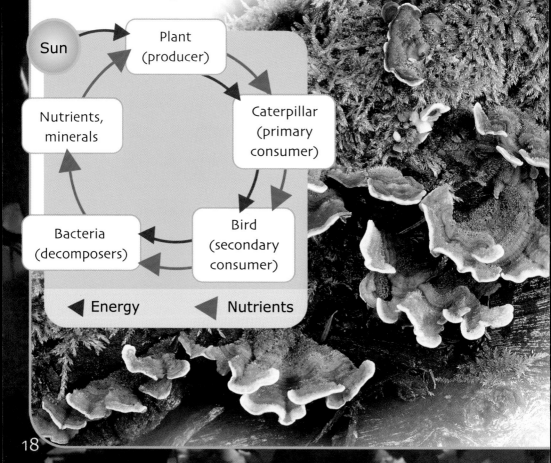

Sun

Plant (producer)

Caterpillar (primary consumer)

Nutrients, minerals

Bacteria (decomposers)

Bird (secondary consumer)

◀ Energy   ◀ Nutrients

Fungi grow on rotting tree trunks and leaf litter. Some fungi are good to eat, but many are poisonous.

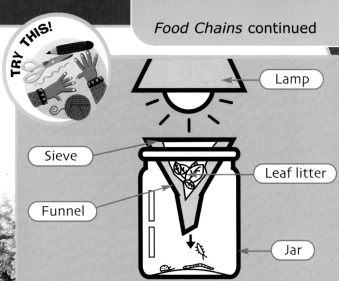

Lamp

Sieve

Leaf litter

Funnel

Jar

Earthworms are decomposers. Some people keep worm farms to make compost.

TRY THIS!

Make a Berlese Funnel

You will need a sieve, a funnel, a jar, and a strong light—an angled lamp is best.

1. Collect some leaf litter. This is the part-leaf, part-soil mixture that you find under trees or by a stream.

2. Pick out the big pieces of leaf, checking for fungus on them.

3. Put the sieve into the funnel set in the jar.

4. Put a small amount of the finer loose litter in the sieve and then shine the light on the top. Any decomposers present will move away from the heat and light, through the sieve, down the funnel, and into the jar.

5. Check the jar after an hour. Can you see tiny animals? These animals are decomposers. Make a chart of what you find, and compare it to what you find in leaf litter from another area.

19

Food Webs

Food webs are overlapping food chains. Food webs can be very large. They describe some or all of the energy transfers in an ecosystem.

Humans are at the top of many food chains, and it takes a lot of food to support us. If we humans had to collect all our own food, competing with our neighbors, we would not be able to have such high population levels. Luckily, humans are able to plan ahead. We can farm plants and animals in the country and transport the food to cities.

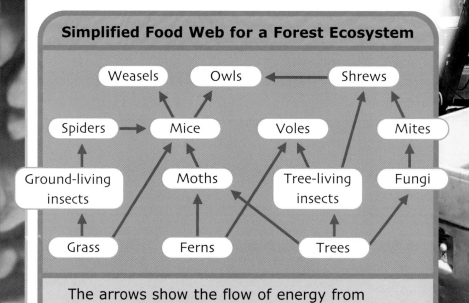

Simplified Food Web for a Forest Ecosystem

The arrows show the flow of energy from the producers to the primary, secondary, and tertiary, or third-level, consumers.

Millions of tons of fish are taken from the oceans every year to feed people.

IN FOCUS

A Link in the Chain

People need to be careful with Earth's resources. Some plants and animals we eat, such as sturgeon fish, are becoming scarce.

Most governments now set rules about which plants and animals people can take from the wild and when they can be taken. The rules are made so that the plant or animal populations have a chance to recover.

Relationships

Many of the relationships between living things are about eating or being eaten, but not all of them are. Some animals work together to the advantage of one another.

Many plants and animals live in groups with others of the same species. Small groups of animals living together are called social groups. Larger groups are known as colonies.

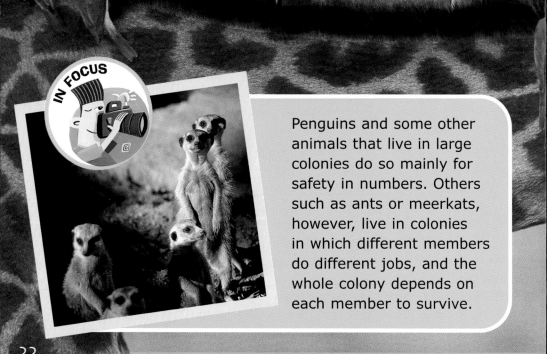

IN FOCUS

Penguins and some other animals that live in large colonies do so mainly for safety in numbers. Others such as ants or meerkats, however, live in colonies in which different members do different jobs, and the whole colony depends on each member to survive.

Symbiosis describes the close relationship between two organisms of different species that live together to their **mutual** advantage. An example of symbiosis is a giraffe and the oxpecker bird which perches on it. The bird eats the insects which irritate the giraffe, so the bird has a source of food while the giraffe gets rid of annoying parasites.

Biodiversity

Extinction is a natural part of the biosphere. Millions of plants and animals have become extinct during the history of Earth, but in the last 300 years, people have caused the extinction of many more species. A few very successful species, such as rats, increase in numbers everywhere, while native plants and animals die out. Because of this, Earth is in danger of losing its **biodiversity.**

Scientists are still discovering how each ecosystem works, but we know already that the loss of one species can have a terrible effect on another. The conservation of plants and animals is vital.

Sometimes a population of animals is too small to save in the wild, so scientists will try to breed the animals in captivity. The best way to save plants and animals, however, is to **conserve** the whole ecosystem.

Weighing these animals is one way scientists can find out more information about all elephants.

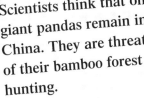

August 21, 1999

Hua Mei

Panda Baby

Animal lovers celebrated today at the announcement of the birth of a baby giant panda at San Diego Zoo. San Diego Zoo's Center for the Reproduction of Endangered Species has been trying to breed a giant panda for a long time—only a few have ever been born in captivity. The newborn has been named Hua Mei.

Scientists think that only about 1,000 giant pandas remain in the wild in China. They are threatened by the loss of their bamboo forest habitat and by hunting.

25

Being Green

Every living thing, including each one of us, affects our biosphere. Some of the greatest damage to ecosystems is done when humans generate power. Nuclear and coal power production both produce large amounts of waste which can pollute ecosystems. Hydroelectric dams can damage the ecosystem of the river downstream.

In Canada and Australia, government organizations are encouraging people and companies to switch to "green power"—electricity that has been generated in an environmentally friendly way.

What Can You Do?

- Put your food scraps into a compost bin so decomposers can recycle them into soil.
- Choose packaging which is less wasteful and **biodegradable.**
- Use less paper, and recycle paper as much as possible.
- Conserve power by turning off lights that you're not using.
- Conserve water.

Some Green Power Options

1. Solar Power

The sun's energy can be used to generate pollution-free energy through solar panels.

2. Landfill and Sewage Gases

Methane gas is produced when waste breaks down in landfills or sewage treatment. This methane is bad for the environment, but it can be burned to make energy.

3. Wind Power

After the cost of the turbine, wind energy is free and there is a never-ending supply. Using wind energy does not pollute the environment.

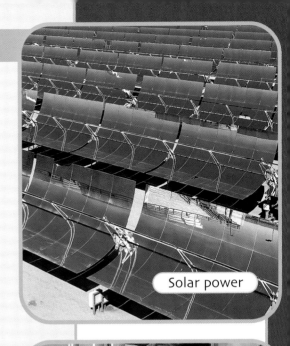

Solar power

Landfill and sewage gases

Wind power

City Living

There are ecosystems everywhere, even in cities. Animals and plants will make themselves at home anywhere they can find enough food and shelter. You'll be amazed at what you see when you look! What plants, birds, and animals can you see in this city ecosystem? Can you figure out a food web? (Answers on page 30)

City Living Answers

1. Pigeons
2. Peregrine falcon
3. Swallow
4. Spider
5. Blue jay
6. Monarch butterfly
7. Cat
8. Gray squirrel
9. Sparrows
10. Turtles
11. Mallard ducks
12. Raccoon
13. Rats
14. Mosquito
15. Dog

An Example Food Web

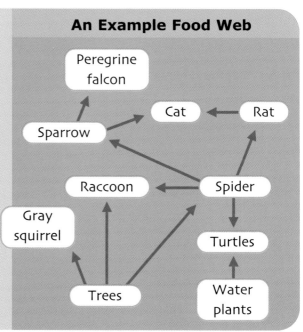

Glossary

biodegradable – able to be broken down by bacteria and other decomposers

biodiversity – the variety of living things in a particular area

conserve – to preserve and look after carefully

mutual – shared or held in common by two or more living things

organism – an animal, a plant, or a single-celled life form

variable – a factor that can be changed in an experiment to see what the effect is

Index

Research Starters

1 People use resources from each of the world's biomes. Find out what we use from each biome. What effects does this use have on those environments?

2 Why are there fewer living things as you move up a food chain? Look at the food chain on page 12. What would happen if a disease killed all the small fish? Look at the food chain on page 18. What would the world be like if there were no decomposers?

3 Biodiversity can be threatened by very successful species such as rats. Can you think of any more examples of successful species? Find out about biodiversity in your region. Are there native plants or animals in your region that are endangered because of a very successful species?

4 How would you and your family cope if there were no supermarkets? Could you hunt or gather your own food? How would this affect your daily life? Find out what others in your family think about this, too.